WILL A MAN ROB GOD?

M. FINLEY-SABIR

WestBow
PRESS
A DIVISION OF THOMAS NELSON

WestBow Press books may be ordered through booksellers or by contacting:

WestBow Press
A Division of Thomas Nelson
1663 Liberty Drive
Bloomington, IN 47403
www.westbowpress.com
1-(866) 928-1240

Because of the dynamic nature of the Internet, any web addresses or links contained in this book may have changed since publication and may no longer be valid. The views expressed in this work are solely those of the author and do not necessarily reflect the views of the publisher, and the publisher hereby disclaims any responsibility for them.

Any people depicted in stock imagery provided by Thinkstock are models, and such images are being used for illustrative purposes only.

Certain stock imagery © Thinkstock.

ISBN: 978-1-4497-2485-6 (sc)
ISBN: 978-1-4497-2484-9 (e)

Library of Congress Control Number: 2011962998

Printed in the United States of America

WestBow Press rev. date: 2/29/2012

I would like to thank Pastor J. Finley for his direction, assistance and guidance from the start of this project. Mainly Pastor J. your recommendations and suggestions are priceless.

Sister Afab, thank you for being there from the start over three years ago. You never stop believing in me.

Special thanks to my friends and family who believed in me and gave me continual support and kept inspiring me to do this.

Finally, words alone cannot convey the thanks I owe to M.A. Sabir, my husband for his encouragement and support.

TABLE OF CONTENTS

SCRIPTURES TO MEDIATE ON

"For Christ is the end of the law for righteousness to everyone that believes" (Romans 10:4 King James Version).

"For Moses describeth the righteousness which is of the law, that the man which doeth those things shall live by them. (Roman 10:5).

"Christ has redeemed us from the curse of the law, being made a curse for us: for it is written, CURSED IS EVERY ONE THAT HANGETH ON A TREE" (Gal. 3:13).

"Therefore then serve the law? It was added because of transgressions, until the seed should come to whom the promise was made; and it was ordained by angels in the hand of a mediator" (Gal. 3:19).

"But before faith came, we were kept under the law, shut up unto the faith which should afterwards be revealed" (Gal. 3:23).

"Therefore the law was our schoolmaster to bring us to Christ, that we might be justified by faith" (Gal. 3:24).

"But after that faith is come, we are no longer under a schoolmaster" (Gal. 3:25).

"For I testify again to every man that is circumcised, that he is a debtor to do the whole law" (Gal. 5:3).

"But if you be led of the Spirit, you are not under the law" (Gal. 5:18).

INTRODUCTION

The information in this book is intended to help the believer have a better understanding of tithing. Hopefully, it will open up the believer's understanding and then allow the believer to make a decision about whether he or she wants to continue to be in bondage or be totally free. It is not intended to change one's belief or practice of tithing. As you read this book, ask God to give you understanding to reveal His word to you so you may know the truth about His word, not man's ideology or man's traditions, but what God truly requires of us as believers. Habits are hard to break, especially if you have been doing something for twenty, thirty, forty years and beyond.

My father was a Pentecostal Pastor and my mother was an Evangelist. I have eight (8) siblings and we were all taught that tithing meant a tenth of our earnings and that we owed God our tithes. We learned that God would not bless us unless we tithed. As a result, I grew up in fear and paranoia, always thinking that God was going to punish me if I didn't pay my tithes or I was disobeying God. As I grew older, I watched so many Christians give their mortgage, rent, and bill money to the church. Like me, they were victims of not clearly understanding the Word of God. I began to realize that our God is a loving and caring God and started to search the scriptures for myself. I never thought about writing a book on tithing until I was told, I couldn't pray for anyone calling in for prayer unless I was a tither. This book expresses what God revealed to me through the Holy Spirit. Three years ago, I was ordained as a License Evangelist in the Pentecostal Church and I want to encourage God's people to read and know the scriptures for themselves, so that they too, can be free and experience the abundant life that God promises to those who trust in Him!

Although most of the scriptures in this book have been typed out, I recommend that you read this book with your Bible.

The Bible says study to show yourself approved unto God a workman that need not be ashamed, rightly dividing the word of truth. I encourage you to be like the Bereans in Acts 17:11; they searched the Scriptures every day to see if what Paul was saying was true.

The Pharisees were good at making themselves look so religious. They were religious, but they had no relationship with God. A perfect example is the Pharisee in Luke 18:12-14 (King James Version), "I fast twice in the week, I give tithes of all that I possess. (v. 13) And the publican, standing afar off, would not lift up so much as his eyes to heaven, but smote upon his breast, saying, God be merciful to me a sinner. (v. 14) I tell you, this man went down to his house justified rather than the other". The tax collector did not profess to be a tither, but he went home justified.

Will a man rob God? This question has been asked in most Pentecostal churches for years during offering time. This often asked question comes from Malachi 3:8 and has been used to convince believers that they owe or are commanded to give God a tithe. As disturbing as this book may be to some, some believers are totally convinced that the only way they can be blessed is to give God a tenth of their earnings. Most believers don't know how blessed they really are or that they are blessed because they are a child of God. What father makes his child pay him in order to receive a gift? What parent would tell his child, if you pay me, I will buy you a house, a car, clothes, a boat, etc., or if you give me a percentage of your earnings, I will leave you an inheritance?

I don't know of any parent that does this to their child. That would be ridiculous. Matthews 7:11 (NIV Study Bible) says, "If you, then though you are evil, know how to give good gifts to your children, how much more shall your Father which is in heaven give good things to them that ask him?" I remember a few years ago, I was told that I could only pray for those who called in for prayer, if I was not a tither. Well, that didn't make sense to me. I couldn't understand how praying for someone equated to tithing. So, I decided to do a study on tithing.

This was probably the best thing I could have ever done. In my studies, I learned there are a plethora of scriptures on tithing, the original intention of tithing, and if tithing is for believers today.

CHAPTER 1:
TITHERS FEEL THEY ARE DISOBEYING GOD IF THEY DON'T PAY THEIR TITHES

Let us explore the scripture, "Will a man rob God?" found in Malachi 3:8. This verse has been quoted during offerings for centuries. Some of you have heard this scripture and have been brainwashed to believe you can only be blessed if you pay your tithes, or you were able to make ends meet because God honored you for paying your tithes, or you needed money and money came in unexpectedly because you paid your tithes. The list goes on as to why believers believe the only way to be blessed by God is to pay their tithes.

You have to wonder, "In order for me to be blessed, I have to pay my tithes, yet the unbeliever does not pay tithes and he is blessed, and other denominations only take an offering and they are blessed." Tithing today is giving a tenth of your gross income, whereas an offering is giving whatever you feel like giving. It is considered a free will offering. The question in my mind is why does the Pentecostal Faith feel its members have to pay tithes in order to be blessed by God? Why do members of the Pentecostal church feel they are disobeying God if they do not pay their tithes? On the one hand, they say they are under grace and truth, but on the other hand, they choose to stay under the curse of the law. They will emphasize the importance of paying tithes, but continue to eat pork. There are plenty of places in the New Testament where Jesus could have emphasized the importance of paying tithes, but He did not. Neither did the disciples of Jesus pay tithes.

Indeed, many Pentecostal ministries have used the tithing element as a method for lining their pockets. Any believer who joins their church is viewed as money, more than a brother or sister of the body of Christ, especially if the new member is a doctor, lawyer, or has a career that pays a good salary. You might hear a pastor say jokingly, "We have Dr. Smith, his tithes will be big," but that pastor really means it.

Will a man rob God? This question continues to echo over the pulpit as Pastors and Ministers prepare their congregation to give their tithes and offerings. However, the emphasis is on the tithing, rather than on both tithes and offerings. Malachi 3:8b says, "But you say, How have we robbed you? In tithes and offerings", (King James Version). Malachi 3:10-11 states:

> "Bring you all of the tithes into the storehouse, that there may be meat in my house, and prove me in this, says the Lord of hosts, see if I will not open you the windows of heaven and pour you out a blessing, that there shall not be room enough to receive it. (v. 11) And I will rebuke the devourer for your sakes, and he shall not destroy the fruits of your ground; neither will your vine cast fruit before the time in the field, says the Lord of hosts."

Let's get an understanding of the tithe. Nowhere in scripture will you read where Moses commanded the children Israel to give money for tithe, because they were to *eat* the tithe. Even in the New Testament (in Matthew 23:23), Jesus tells the **teachers of the Law and Pharisees** they are hypocrites because they would give a tenth of their spices—mint, dill and cumin—yet they neglected important matters of the law: justice, mercy and faithfulness.

God never intended for the tithe to be money. In fact, tithes were supposed to be grain, fruit, herd and flock. According to Leviticus 27:30-32,

> "All the tithe from the land, the seeds from the land, or grain from the soil or fruit from the trees, were the Lord's: it was holy to the Lord. And if a man was to redeem his tithes, he was obligated to add a fifth of the value to it. The tithe of the herd or of the flock; whatever went under the rod, the tenth or every tenth animal was holy to the Lord."

The tithe was considered a sacred meal offered once a year. According to Mosaic Law, only the owners of farms and flocks were required to tithe. It is also important to note that this law was ordained for Israel only. To say God requires or commands you to pay ten percent in the 21st century is inaccurate. Pastors will tell you to give God his first and then the rest belongs to you. This does not coincide with Leviticus 27:32. Let's read this verse again: "And concerning the tithe of the herd, or of the flock, even of whatsoever pass under the rod, the tenth shall be holy unto the Lord." Only the tenth sheep or calf or goat was holy to the Lord: not money. People did use money back then, but it was atonement money for the souls of the children of Israel. As it is written in Exodus 30:16, The Lord told Moses to take the atonement money from the children of Israel, and designate it for service of the tabernacle of the congregation; it was to be a memorial to the children of Israel before the LORD; an atonement for their souls.

To further understand, tithes were to be eaten; carpenters, silversmiths, craftsmen, perfumers, bakers, confectioners, barbers, chamberlains, engravers, goldsmiths, masons, merchants, potters, and widows were not required to pay tithes. (1 Samuel 8:13, talks about bakers, confectioners, and cooks). Actually, the tithes were for the widows. Today, widows are encouraged by some Pastors to give a tenth of their fixed income.

Some Pastors, Ministers, and Evangelists teach that God must get his money first. But according to the Bible, "the tenth animal that passed under the shepherd's rod" belonged to God. I have heard some Ministers say, the only way God can know if he can really trust you, is for you to pay your tithes. The children Israel tithing was not based on God wanting to know if he could really trust them, but their tithing did three things: 1) It was God's blessing plan for the children Israel of always having plenty and never lacking 2) It allowed them to fellowship with God 3) It gave glory to God by them giving their tithes to the Levites, the stranger, the fatherless, and the widow. God needs to be able to trust us with something more valuable than tithing/money. He needs to know he can trust you with His word.

If tithing were implemented today as it was during Biblical times, a believer would be required to pay approximately fifteen to twenty percent, instead of ten percent. In Leviticus 27:31, If a man was to redeem any of his tithe, he had to add a fifth to the value of it. In the Old Testament, holiness was described as a divine call or ceremony. It required the total consecration of a man's life to God's service, which involved giving one's self, one's family, and all of one's possessions to God.

CHAPTER 2:
FLOODGATES OF HEAVEN

When the Lord said he would open up the "floodgates of heaven" in Malachi 3:10 NIV, he was speaking about the storehouse in the heavens which holds the rain. If the people were to keep the covenant and offer up healthy animals, not injured, blind, crippled, and diseased animals, to the Lord, the floodgates of heaven would be opened, allowing so much rain to fall on the land there would be an abundance of crops. Deuteronomy 28:12 NIV puts it this way, "The Lord will open the heavens, the storehouse of his bounty, to send rain on your land in season and to bless all the work of your hands . . ."

Malachi 3:10-11 (NIV) describes the opposite of being under a curse for not obeying God's law. God promises to open the floodgates of heaven and pour out an abundance of blessing (in the form of crops) in exchange for those devoted to paying their tithes. According to Deuteronomy 28:12, The Lord would open to the children of Israel his good treasure, the heaven (storehouse) and give rain in the land in its season, and to bless all the work of their hand: and they would be in a position to lend to many nations, but never borrow.

If the children of Israel obeyed God, He would prevent the pest from eating their crops. Malachi 3:11 KJV says, "And I will rebuke the devourer for your sakes, and he shall not destroy the fruits of your ground; neither shall your vine cast her fruit before the time in the field, says the Lord of hosts." God would stop pests from eating the children of Israel crops, and he would not destroy the fruit of their ground, and their vines would not reproduce fruit before its time in the field. This prevention was based on Israel obeying God and storing the tithe [food] in the storehouse so there could be food [not money] in his house. If they obeyed him, they would not have to worry about being under the curse any longer. The curse was not being able to gather their grapes because worms would eat them, and not being able to use the olives because they would fall off the vine before they were ripe (read Deut. 28:39-40).

Somehow Bishops and Pastors and mainly the Pentecostal faith are able to take Malachi 3:10 as meaning money and then impose this as a law, duty, or command upon believers. This scripture was never meant for the tithe to be a substitute for money. The Bible clearly says the tithes were to be eaten. The tithe was also God's way of providing food for the Priests, the Levites, the widow, the orphan, and the stranger. The custom of tithing was strictly for God's people Israel and not for Gentiles. It was used as a festive meal and brought to a holy place the Lord would choose as a dwelling place for his name. This was God's way of having fellowship with his people Israel. This typology was an indication of the fellowship we would have with our Savior Jesus Christ, who is the bread of life.

According to Baker Reference Library Evangelical Dictionary of Theology 2nd Edition (Elwell, 2001); In the sixteenth and seventeenth century in England, tithing were a source of intense conflict; because a state church depended on tithes for its living. The Archbishop Laud tried to increase tithe payments prior to 1640. But the English Puritans and others wanted the tithes eliminated and support clergy through voluntary contributions. At that time, the questions of tithing aroused some fierce and bitter issues, which were associated with the English Civil War. Tithing survived in England until the twentieth century. (Elwell, p.1203)

CHAPTER 3:
WHAT WAS IT?

What was a tithe? It was grain, new wine and oil, and the firstborn of cattle. Deuteronomy 14:23 states,

> "And thou shalt eat before the Lord thy God, in the place which he shall choose to place his name there, the tithe of thy corn, of thy wine, and of thine oil, and the firstlings of thy herds and of thy flocks; that thou mayest learn to fear the Lord thy God always.

Scriptures after scriptures denotes **tithes** as being something to eat and not money. The exception to this is when Abram gave Melchizedek, king of Salem a tenth of the plunder after Abram defeated Kedorlaomer and the king's who were with him. Melchizedek blessed Abram and Abram gave him a tenth of everything. Abram knew the custom of giving tithes to kings and understood that a tenth was a king's share. We will discuss this later. God made a covenant with Abram and told him if he could count the stars in the heavens, "so shall your offspring be" (Read Gen. 14:17-24, 15:5).

In the book of Deuteronomy, you will read the tithe as something to eat. Deuteronomy 12:17-18 (NIV Study Bible) states, "You must not eat in your own towns the tithe of your grain, and new wine, and oil . . ." (v. 18) instead you are to eat them in the presence of the Lord your God at the place the Lord your God will choose." Numbers 18:31 states, "You and your households may eat the rest of it anywhere, for it is your wages for your work at the Tent of Meeting." Deuteronomy 14:28-29 (King James Version) reads,

> At the end of every three years thou shalt bring forth all the tithe of thine increase the same year, and shalt lay it up within thy gates: (v. 29) And the Levite, (because he hath no inheritance with thee), and the stranger, and the fatherless and the widows, which are within thy gates, shall come, and eat and be satisfied; that the Lord thy God may bless you in all the work of thine hand which thou doest.

Now let's read Deuteronomy 14:26 NIV, "Use the silver to buy whatever you like: cattle, sheep, wine or other fermented drink, or anything you wish. Then you and your household shall eat there in the presence of the Lord your God and rejoice." You can see the value God placed on fellowshipping with his people Israel.

Jesus would often engaged in fellowship with his disciples by eating bread and drinking wine with them. His last fellowship with the disciples was the last or Lord's Supper. Mark 14:22-23 KJV states, "And as they did eat, Jesus took bread, and blessed, and brake it, and gave to them, and said, Take, eat: this is my body. (v. 23) And he took the cup, and when he had given thanks, he gave it to them: and they all drank from it."

It is ironic that most of these scriptures are never preached by Pastors, Ministers, Evangelist, or Missionaries. I have been in the Pentecostal denomination all my life, over 45 years and I never heard a message preached from the book of Deut. 12:17-18, 14:26, 14:28-29, and Num. 18:31. You see, to preach on these scriptures, one would have to preach about the tithe being something to eat and the type of foods that were required as the tithe. Could it be that they know the truth about the tithe, but want to keep us blinded and in bondage?

Some things don't make sense; in order to be blessed, you have to pay tithes, yet sinners do not pay tithes and they are blessed. They live in nice homes, drive nice cars, have money in the bank, and own businesses without ever paying tithes. But if you are a child of God and you want a car, house, bank account, riches, or what ever you desire, you pay God first and then you can acquire these things. What parents does this to their children? It doesn't make sense. I realized the key to my success or blessings is to seek first the kingdom of God and then all these things would be given to me, read Matt. 6:33. If you have a good career or make some good investments, you can have the better things in life. I knew a millionaire who owned several businesses, homes, and cars and attended one of the largest churches in a certain city; he never paid tithes, but gave an offering. He was a giver and a big one at that, but not of tithes. He would give large sums of money to help senior citizens. He loved the Lord and understood the principle of giving and he new how to make money.

Now, let's read Deuteronomy 12:1 (NIV Study Bible), "These are the decrees and laws you must be careful to follow in the land that the Lord, the God of your fathers, has given you to possess—*as long as you live in the land.*" These decrees and laws were to be followed or obeyed as long as the children of Israel lived in the land of Canaan. Israel later disobeyed these decrees and laws and worshipped other gods. Because of their disobedience, the Lord allowed them to be taken in exile into Babylon. The practice of the law was no longer valid; it was only valid as long as the Israelites lived in the land of Canaan. We will discuss this again later when we explore how the scribes and Pharisees re-instated the law for their gain.

CHAPTER 4:
THE LAW, THE JEWS, & THE GENTILES

The number of followers of Jesus Christ increased greatly. Acts 6:7 (King James Version) reads, "And the word of God increased; and a large number of the disciples multiplied in Jerusalem greatly; and priests were obedient to the faith." This passage describes priests who were believers in the Lord Jesus Christ and at the same time continued as priests of the altar and ordinances of the law.

The Pharisees believed Gentiles believers should be circumcised just like the Jews were circumcised according to the Law. Acts 15:5 (KJV) reads, "But there rose up certain of the sect of the Pharisees which believed, saying, that it was needful to circumcise them, and to command them to keep the Law of Moses." A certain sect of the Pharisees insisted this practice be done on Gentiles who accepted Jesus as their Savior. These Pharisees did not understand that the Lord required a circumcision of the heart and not of the physical body. Our hearts can only be circumcised through the word of God, "For the word of God is quick, and powerful, and sharper than any two edged sword, piercing even to the dividing asunder of the soul and spirit, and of the joints and marrow, and is a discerner of the thoughts and intents of the heart" (Heb. 4:12).

Many Jews believed in the Lord Jesus, but they were still practicing the rituals of the Law. Acts 21:20 describes thousands of Jews that believed and were zealous about the law. We must understand that grace and the law are opposites. Salvation is by faith, but salvation of the Mosaic Law is by works. The Mosaic Law made the children of Israel aware of their sins, but it could not keep them from sinning. In the Old Testament, the children of Israel salvation was based on the law and not faith in Jesus Christ. To be clear, salvation has nothing to do with tithing. Tithing is of the law and therefore it is considered a part of "good works." Thousands of Jews had come to believe in Jesus as the Messiah, but knew little of him as Savior. They were still "zealous of the law" in that they had not forsaken Moses by giving up circumcision, continuing with their traditions, and still offering "sacrifices." Paul's teachings were contrary to the law and caused such hostility among some of the believers that the Pharisees desired to kill him. "James and the elders" feared the hostility from the crowd because there were thousands in the crowd and all were not Jews, but from the thousands that believed.

Paul informs the Jewish believers that the Gentiles were not being required to practice Jewish rituals. Acts 21:24-25 says, "Them take, and purify thyself with them, and be at charges with them, that they may shave their heads: and all may know that those things, whereof they were informed concerning thee, are nothing; but that thou thyself also walk orderly, and keepest the law. (v. 25) As for touching the Gentiles which believe, we have written and concluded that they observe no such thing, save only that they keep themselves from things offered to idols, and from blood, and from strangled, and from fornication." Paul is very clear, he did not want Gentiles believers to practice any Jewish rituals or the keeping of the Mosaic Law, except to keep from things offered to idols, from blood, from strangled, and from fornication.

Paul's life among the Jews was one of accommodation. When he was with the Jews, he became a Jew. He would pay the temple fee, not tithes, and purify himself with the Jews. He demonstrated that he was not hostile toward the Mosaic Law or the Jews who observed it. Paul never mentioned to the Gentiles about paying tithes because he knew our high priest had died on the cross and rose from the dead and is now seated at the right hand of the Father. Paul was careful not to impose the law on Christian principle. Paul asked the Galatians (Gal. 3:2), "Did you receive the Spirit by observing the law, or by believing what you heard?" Some rituals were observed by the Jewish Christians and some were not. Gentiles were not required to observe the Jewish rituals or the Mosaic Law.

In the beginning of Acts 22, Paul explains his position as being born a Jew in Tarsus of Cilicia, brought up in Jerusalem and taught at the feet of Gamaliel. Gamaliel was the most honored rabbi of the First Century. Paul was thoroughly trained according to the law of their fathers, Abraham, Isaac, and Jacob. He persecuted those followers of Jesus Christ, both men and women, some were killed and some were thrown in prison. However, while on his way to Damascus, he met Jesus and was regenerated or born again. The Lord sent him far away to the Gentiles. Paul was focused; he preached about Jesus, the love of Jesus, the mercies of God, loving one another, and giving to others. Throughout Paul's ministry you will never read where Paul commanded the Gentiles to tithe. Rather, he always encouraged giving both sparingly and cheerfully.

Paul understood those who believed in Jesus Christ were no longer in bondage, he understood God wanted people to give willingly and not begrudgingly or reluctantly. In my opinion, if you tithe because you feel this is what you have been taught to do but are not doing so willingly, God does not want your tithes or your offerings because they are not from the heart. Paul puts it this way in Romans 7:6, But now we are delivered from the law, that being dead wherein we were held; that we should serve in newness of spirit, and not in the oldness of the letter. The law, which once bound believers can no longer keep them bound because they are released from the law through the blood of Jesus Christ. Believers no longer have to practice the religious rituals of the Mosaic Law. They can now go directly to God without having to go to the Priest for their sins and without having to sacrifice something for their sins. Remember, salvation is by faith, but salvation of the Mosaic Law is by good works.

Paul was into winning souls: He was free from all men, yet he made himself a servant to all, that he might reach more. To the Jew he became a Jew; that he might reach the Jew, to those under the law, as under the law, that he might reach them under the law.

To those that were without the law, as without the law; that he might reached those without the law. (Read 1 Cor. 9:19-21).

Paul clearly makes the distinction between those who were Jews, those under the law, and those not having the law. There were those Jews who did not practice the Mosaic Law, those who practice the Mosaic Law, and those who were Gentiles or non Jew.

The word Jew does not occur before the period of Jeremiah. Originally it meant "one belonging to the tribe of Judah." Later, it meant anyone of the Hebrew race who returned from the Babylonian Captivity, most of those in exile came from Judah. Finally, the term Jew was understood to mean all of the Hebrews throughout the world.

CHAPTER 5:
POST EXILE—THE REMENANT

The Jewish legalism began after the Babylonian captivity. The Temple worship and sacrifices had terminated and Judaism began to center its activities in Jewish Law and the synagogue. The Pharisees were the religious leaders of the Jews. The Pharisees were the "separated ones" after the Babylonian Captivity. (Elwell, p. 913) They became a secluded organized group: very loyal to society and each other, but separated from others, including their own people. The Pharisees main concern was the observance of purity and tithing laws.

Around the tenth chapter of 1 Kings, we see Israel asking for a king. Samuel was displeased with the children of Israel because they wanted a new king instead of allowing God to continue to be their King. But God told him to listen to the people because they had not rejected him but instead rejected God as their king. Israel wanted to be like other nations who had a king to rule over them. Israel had several kings, but King Solomon was the wealthiest one. His wealth was not because the children of Israel paid tithes to him, but rather because of the talents of gold he received yearly as revenue from merchants, traders, and all the Arabian kings and the governors of the land (read 1 Kings 10:14).

Israel had a census tax originated by Moses when they crossed over the Red Sea. This money was used for the service of the Tent of Meeting. It was also called the sanctuary shekel. In 2 Kings, chapter 12, we learn there were three sources derived for collecting money:

1. The census money, which was collected from Israelite youth of 20 years old who were required to register for military service (read Ex.30:11-16; 38:25-26). Even Jesus paid the annual temple tax, which was two drachmas (approximately two days wages) and was used for the upkeep of the temple;
2. Money received from personal vows (read Lev. 27:1-25);

3. Money brought voluntarily to the temple, voluntary offerings (read Lev. 22:18-23; Deut. 16:10). This money was used to repair damages found in the temple.

When Joash was King of Judah, he decided to restore the temple of the Lord; he gathered the priests and Levites and told them to go down to Judah and collect the annual money that was due from all of Israel. This money was used to repair the temple of God. A proclamation was issued in Judah and Jerusalem for the children of Israel to bring the Lord the tax that Moses had originally required of Israel in the desert. All the people and officials brought their contributions gladly. Masons, carpenters, and workers in iron and bronze were hired to repair the temple. With the money collected they rebuilt the temple of God according to its original design.

Although Malachi is the last book in the Old Testament, Malachi does not give a date to his prophecy; however, there are events to the estimated time of it. It was post-exilic and after the other two post-exilic prophets, Haggai and Zechariah. It was most likely written later than the days of Nehemiah. The important dates and events relating to the Jewish remnant are those 50,000 Jews that survived the Babylon exile and who returned to Judea: The time frame from when the children of Israel returned to Judea down to the ministry of Malachi are as follows:

536 B.C.—50,000 returned to Judea under Zerubbabel, read Ezra chapter 1 and 2. (Baxter, p. 259)

534 B.C.—The foundation for the new temple was laid, read Ezra chapter 3. (Baxter, p. 259)

520 B.C.—Haggai and Zechariah prophesies to the Jews that were in Judah and Jerusalem. The temple building is resumed, read Ezra chapter 5; Haggai 1:15. (Baxter, p. 259)

516 B.C.—Twenty years after the 50,000 returned, the restoration of the temple is completed, read Ezra 6:15. (Baxter, p. 260)

457 B.C.—Under Ezra 1,800 men returned, plus wives, daughters and servants, read Ezra chapter 7. (Baxter, p. 260)

445 B.C.—Nehemiah comes to Jerusalem as Governor to re-build the city, read Nehemiah Chapter 2. (Baxter, P. 260)

430 B.C.—Mahachi prophesies sometime after his visit to Artaxerxes, read Neh. 8:6 &7. (Baxter, p. 260)

It is clear that by the time of the prophecy of Malachi 3:10, the reinstatement of tithing was after Israel's return from the Babylonian Exile. Those who returned were the Jewish remnant: approximately 51,800 Jewish men, plus wives, daughters, and servants. (The book of Ezra gives a list of those who came up from captivity of the exiles, whom Nebuchadnezzar, King of Babylon had taken captive to Babylon; later, these Jews returned to Jerusalem and Judah). Ezra 2:1, 64-65, "Now these are the children of the province that went up out of the captivity, of those which had been carried away, whom Nebuchadnezzar the king of Babylon had carried away unto Babylon, and came again unto Jerusalem and Judah, every one unto his city. (v. 64) "The whole congregation together was forty and two thousand three hundred and threescore, (v.65) Beside their servants and their maids, of whom there were seven thousand three hundred thirty and seven; and there were among them two hundred singing men and singing women."

Nehemiah 10:37-39 describes how, after 458 B.C., a smaller city was built in Jerusalem and a temple with new walls was constructed. The people assembled in the square before the water gate and told Ezra to bring out the book of Law of Moses, which the Lord had commanded for Israel. The Israelite's were taught that day was holy unto the Lord and not to mourn or weep. The people had been weeping as the Law was read. They were regretful for their failures and those of their ancestors. Nehemiah said to them " . . . Go your way, eat the fat, and drink the sweet, and send portions unto them for whom nothing is prepared: for this day is holy unto our Lord: neither be ye sorry; for the joy of the Lord is your strength" (Neh. 8:10).

In chapter 10 of Nehemiah, the people made a binding agreement to follow the Law of God given through Moses the servant of God and to obey carefully all the commandments, regulations, and decrees of the Lord. One of the commandments was to assume the responsibility to give a third of a shekel each year for the service of the house of God. Originally, it was a half shekel as an offering to the Lord. This was to be done by each man aged 20 years and older as a symbolic ransom of Jesus dying on the cross and redeeming man back to God. King Joash of Judah used annual contributions to repair the temple. In the New Testament, Jewish men everywhere sent an offering of a half shekel or two drachmas, which would be the same as a day's wages. Due to the economical situation, meaning the poverty of the children of Israel during Nehemiah's time, a third shekel may have been required instead of the full half shekel.

The children of Israel believed their salvation was based upon good works and accepted the Old Testament Scriptures, and encouraged the Jewish messianic hope.

CHAPTER 6:
THE PHARISEES AND JESUS

It was destined that the Pharisees would bitterly oppose Jesus and his teaching in John 9:16 and 22. Verse 16 states, "Therefore said some of the Pharisees, This man is not from God, because he keep not the sabbath day. Others said, How can a man that is a sinner do such miracles? And there was a division among them." Verse 22 states, "These words spoke his parents, because they feared the Jews: for the Jews had agreed already, that if any man did confess that he was Christ, he should be put out of the synagogue."

The conflict between Jesus and the Pharisees were frequent and bitter, as reflected in the following verses:

- "But when he saw many of the Pharisees and Sadducees come to his baptism, he said unto them, O generation of vipers, who has warned you to flee from the wrath to come" (Matt. 3:7)?
- "For I say unto you, that except your righteousness shall exceed the righteousness of the scribes and Pharisees, ye shall in no case enter into the kingdom of heaven" (Matt. 5:20).
- "But the Pharisees said, He casteth out devils through the prince of the devils" (Matt. 9:34).
- "But when the Pharisees saw it, they said to him, 'Behold, thy disciples do that which is not lawful to do on the Sabbath day" (Matt. 12:2).
- "And the scribes and the Pharisees began to reason, saying, Who is this which speaketh blasphemies? Who can forgive sins, but God alone" (Luke 5:21)?
- "But the Pharisees and lawyers rejected the counsel of God against themselves, being not baptized of him" (Luke 7:30).
- "And the Pharisees also, who were covetous, heard all these things: and they derided him" (Luke 16:14).

Jesus' longest rebuke of the Pharisees is found in Matthew 23:13-39. I will only write out verses 13-16, "But woe unto you, scribes and Pharisees, hypocrites! for ye shut up the kingdom of heaven against men: for ye neither go in yourselves, neither suffer ye them that are entering to go in. (v. 14) Woe unto you, scribes and Pharisees, hypocrites! for ye devour widows' houses, and for a pretense make long prayer: therefore ye shall receive the greater damnation. (v. 15) Woe unto you, Scribes and Pharisees, hypocrites! for ye compass sea and land to make one proselyte, and when he is made, ye make him twofold more the child of hell than yourselves. (v. 16) Woe unto you ye blind guides, which say, Whosoever shall swear by the temple, it is nothing; but whosoever shall swear by the gold of the temple, he is a debtor!

In the New Testament, the Pharisees were not a positive group. Jesus condemned the Pharisees' too presumptuous, their salvation by works, their hypocrisy, and their unpleasantness. Not all Pharisees were this way; some were members of the Christian movement in the beginning: "And the word of God increased; and the number of the disciples multiplied in Jerusalem greatly; and a great company of the priests were obedient to the faith" (Acts 6:7). Some of the greatest men of the New Testament were Pharisees, including Nicodemus "There was a man of the Pharisees, named Nicodemus, a ruler of the Jews" (John 3:1), Gamaliel "A Pharisee named Gamaliel, a doctor of the law . . ." (Acts 5:34), and Paul "Circumcised on the eighth day, of the stock of Israel, of the tribe of Benjamin, a Hebrew of Hebrews; as touching the law, a Pharisee; Concerning zeal, persecuting the church; touching the righteousness which is in the law, blameless" (Philippians 3:5-6). Paul did not think of himself has a hypocrite, but claimed the highest degree of faithfulness to the law.

CHAPTER 7:
WHERE DID TITHING COME FROM?

The idea of making ten percent the rate for paying tribute to rulers and offering gifts as a religious obligation is unknown. However, history reveals that it existed in ancient Babylon, Persia, Egypt, and China. Abraham knew of it when he emigrated from Ur, the land of the Chaldeans which was the early home of Abraham. Genesis 11:27-28 states, "Now these are the generations of Terah: Terah begat Abram, Nahor and Haran; and Haran begat Lot. (v. 28) And Haran died before his father Terah in the land of his nativity, in Ur of the Chaldees." Ur is located in Southern Mesopotamia: approximately 140 miles southeast of Babylon.

Abraham knew and was aware of the religious customs of giving tithes to the kings. Genesis 14:17 says, "And the king of Sodom went out to meet him after his return from the slaughter of Chedorlaomer, and of the kings that were with him, at the valley of shaveh, which is the king's dale. (Chedorlaomer is located south of Media and east of Babylonia.) He was raised in a region where tithing was practiced as a holy deed. So when Melchizedek, who was king of Salem, brought him bread and wine and blessed him, Abram knew to give him a tenth of everything from the spoils or plunder taken from the enemy in war. As it is written in Genesis 14:18-20, "And Melchizedek king of Salem brought out bread and wine: and he was priest of most high God. (v. 19) And he blessed him, and said, Blessed be Abram of the most high God, possessor of heaven and earth. (v. 20) And blessed be the most high God, which hath delivered thine enemies into thine hand. And he gave him tithes of all." Since Melchizedek was a priest of the Most High, it is certain that in Abraham's day the giving of tithes was recognized as a ***holy deed*** (read Heb. 7:4).

Abraham's paying tithes to Melchizadeck was a shadow and typology of what was to come, specifically regarding the Jewish nation's choice to reject God as their leader and select an earthly king. Although God called Noah a righteous man; there is no occurrence of tithing from Adam to Noah. Deuteronomy 5:2-3 says, "The Lord our God made a covenant with us in Horeb. (v. 3) The Lord made not this covenant with our fathers, but with us, even us, who are all of us here alive this day." **The original Ten Commandments**, found in Exodus 20:1-17, does not mention tithing. Nowhere in the scriptures do we find that Noah was not blessed by God or was barred from entering heaven because he did not tithe to God. In fact, God made a covenant with Noah; God called Noah righteous, he found grace in God's eyes, he is called a just man, and was considered perfect in his generation. He walked with God and never paid any tithes. Genesis 9:1 says, "And God blessed Noah and his sons." Noah performed priestly duties by building an Alter unto the Lord and offering clean beasts and fowl as a burnt offering (read Gen. 8:20). Noah represents gentile believer's, he was not a part of the Levitical priesthood.

If we look at the book of Job, he also performed daily priestly duties and offered burnt offerings to God to sanctify his children (see Job 1:5). Many biblical scholars believe that Job lived in the patriarchal days before the Levitical priesthood was established. According to Job 1:1, Job was a perfect and upright man who feared God. There is no record of Job paying tithes. After he had lost all of his possessions, we read that not only was he blessed, Job. 42:12 says, "So the Lord blessed the latter end of Job more than his beginning: for he had fourteen thousand sheep, and six thousand camels, and a thousand yoke of oxen, and a thousand she asses." You will never read that Job was cursed by God because he did not tithe. As with Noah, it is not recorded in the Bible that Job was not allowed to enter heaven because he did not pay tithes. Neither of these men, were under the Law of Moses: during their lifetime of service to God. Yet they were abundantly blessed by God and entered into a perpetual covenant with God; Noah's was symbolized by the rainbow.

I believe that Noah and Job are certainly in heaven right now and will not be thrown out on the great judgment day.

Jacob recognized the Lord as his God and King and vowed to give God a tenth of all God would give him. Jacob vowed to do this, provided the Lord return him safely back to the place he called Bethel. In Genesis 28:18-22 it is written:

> And Jacob rose up early in the morning, and took the stone that he had put for his pillows, and set it up for a pillar, and poured oil upon the top of it. (v. 19) And he called the name of that place Bethel: but the name of that city was called Luz at first. (v. 20) And Jacob vowed a vow, saying, If God will be with me, and will give me bread to eat, and raiment to put on, (v. 21) So that I come again to my father's house in peace; then shall the Lord be my God: (v. 22) And this stone, which I have set for a pillar, shall be God's house: and of all that you will give me I will surely give the tenth unto you.

The vow was *voluntary* on Jacob's part, because God had not commanded it.

Abram's "tenth" to Melchizedek was voluntary too. Tithing was not required until the Law was given to Israel.

CHAPTER 8:
WHO WAS EXEMPT FROM
PAYING TITHES?

The tithes of the land and the fruit of the tree were holy to the Lord and all of the tithes of Israel were given to the children of Levi for their inheritance. Leviticus 27:30 says, "And all the tithe of the land, whether of the seed of the land, or of the fruit of the tree, is the Lord's: it is holy unto the Lord." Furthermore, Numbers 18:21 states, "And, behold, I have given the children of Levi all the tenth in Israel for an inheritance, for their service of the service of the tabernacle of the congregation."

Deuteronomy 14:22 states, "You shall truly tithe all the increase of thy seed, that the field bring forth year by year." According to Deuteronomy 14:29, tithing did not apply to all of the Israelites. Among those to whom tithing did not apply were the poor Levites who had no inheritance of their own, the fatherless, widows, and strangers. At the end of the third year of tithing, the tithes were gathered in the towns and stored for distribution to the poor Levites and the less fortunate, who would then eat the tithes.

Again, the children of Israel were commanded to pay tithes as long as they lived in the promise land. Deuteronomy 12:1 reads, ***"These are the statutes and judgments, which ye shall observe to do in the land, which the Lord God of thy fathers giveth thee to possess it, all the days that you live upon the earth (land)."***

The children of Israel had begun complaining they wanted a king like the other nations. So Samuel warned the children of Israel, that a king would obtain tithes of their grain and flocks: "He will take the tenth of your grain and of your vintage and give to his officers and attendants" (1 Samuel 8:15).

CHAPTER 9:
WHO WERE THE TITHES FOR?

It was a long time before legal requirements were set regarding tithing. As a result, customs for paying tithes were diverse. At first the tithes were intended for the Levites. Numbers 18:21 states, "And, behold, I have given the children of Levi all the tenth in Israel for an inheritance, for their service which they serve, even the service of the tabernacle of the congregation." Tithing was provided for the tribe of Levi and was considered payment for their service, even the service of the tabernacle of the congregation. Deuteronomy 14:22-29, also known as "The Law of the Tithe," reads,

> Thou shalt truly tithe all the increase of thy seed, that the field bringeth forth year after year." Farmers produced crop once a year. (v. 23) And thy shalt eat before the Lord thy God, in the place which he shall choose to place his name there, the tithe of thy corn, of thy wine, and of thine oil, and the firstlings of thy herds and of thy flocks; that thou mayest learn to fear the Lord thy God always. (v. 24) And if the way be too long for thee, so that thou are not able to carry it; or if the place be too far from thee, which the Lord thy God shall choose to set his name there, when the Lord thy God has blessed you: (v. 25) Then shalt thy turn it into money, and bind up the money in thine hand, and shalt go unto the place which the Lord thy God shall choose; (v. 26) And thou shalt bestow that money for whatsoever thou soul lust after, for oxen, or for sheep, or for wine, or for strong drink, or for whatsoever thy soul desire: and thou shalt eat there before the Lord thy God, and thy shalt rejoice, thou and thine household. (v. 27) And the Levite that is within thy gates; thou shalt not forsake him; for he hath no part nor inheritance with thee. (v. 28) At the end of three years thou shalt bring forth all the tithe of thine increase the same year, and shalt lay it up within thy gates: (v. 29) And the Levite, (because he hath no part nor inheritance with thee), and the stranger, and the

fatherless, and the widow, which are within thy gates shall come, and shall eat and be satisfied; that the Lord thy God may bless thee in all the work of thine hand which you do.

After the Levitical code had been established, tithes belonged exclusively to the Levites. A penalty of fifteen percent of the tithe was taken from one who sold his tithes and refused to use the money to pay for a substitute: "If a man redeems any of his tithe, he must add a fifth of the value to it" (Lev. 27:31 NIV). The Levites in turn gave a tenth of their grain, fruit, and of their herd or flock to provide for the priests:

This is what the LORD spoke to Moses, (v. 26) "Thus speak unto the Levites, and say unto them, When ye take of the children of Israel the tithes which I have given you from them for your inheritance, then ye shall offer up an heave offering of it for the Lord, even a tenth part of the tithe. (v. 27) And this your heave offering shall be reckoned unto you, as though it were the corn of the threshing floor, and as the fullness of the winepress. (v. 28) Thus ye also shall offer a heave offering unto the Lord of all your tithes, which ye receive of the children of Israel; and ye shall give thereof the Lord's heave offering to Aaron the priest. (v. 29) Out of all your gifts ye shall offer every heave offering of the Lord, of all the best thereof, even the hallowed part thereof out of it. (v. 30) Therefore thou shalt say to them, 'When ye have heaved the best thereof from it, then it shall be counted unto the Levites as the increase of the threshing floor, and as the increase of the winepress. (v. 31) And ye shall eat in every place, ye and your households; for it is your reward for your service in the tabernacle of the congregation. (v. 32) And ye shall bear no sin by reason of it, when ye have heaved from it the best of it; neither shall ye pollute the holy things of the children of Israel, lest ye die. (Num. 18:25-32)

The Israelites were to give the Lord the best parts of all their earthly goods, which would be given to Aaron the priest. The temple was the place to which tithes were taken:

> But unto the place which the Lord your God shall choose out of all your tribes to put his Name there, even unto his habitation shall ye seek, and thither thou shalt come (v. 6) And thither ye shall bring your burnt offerings, and your sacrifices, and your tithes, and heave (raise) offerings of your hand, and your vows, and your freewill offerings, and the firstlings of your herds and of your flock: (v. 7) And there ye shall eat before the Lord your God, and ye shall rejoice in all that ye put your hand unto, ye and your households, wherein the Lord thou God hath blessed thee. (v. 8) Ye shall not do after all the things that we do here this day. Every man whatsoever is right in his own eyes. (v. 9) For ye are not as yet come to the rest and to the inheritance, which the Lord your God gives you. (v. 10) But when ye go over to Jordan, and dwell in the land which the Lord your God giveth you to inherit, and when he giveth you rest from your enemies around about, so that ye dwell in safety; (v. 11) Then there shall be a place which the Lord your God shall choose to cause his name to dwell there, thither shall ye bring all that I command you; your burnt offerings, and your sacrifices, your tithes, and the heave offering of your hand, and all your choice vows which ye vow unto the Lord: (Notice the different offerings the children of Israel was required to bring.) (v. 12) And ye shall rejoice before the LORD your God, ye, your sons and daughters, your menservants and maidservants, and the Levites that is within your gates; forasmuch as he hath no part nor inheritance with you. (Deut 12:5-12)

Again, in verse 12 there is no mentioning of widows, orphans, or strangers. They were excluded from tithing and from the dwelling place the Lord chose for the Israelites.

It is important to understand that God chose the place where the Israelites were to bring the tithes; this was a place where he would put His name and the place the tithe would be eaten. It was to be a place of communion, relationship, a place of fellowship, and a place of thanksgiving.

The time to give tithes to the widows, orphans, and strangers came every third year:

> At the end of every three years thou shalt bring forth all the tithe of thine increase the same year, and shalt lay it up within thy gates: (v. 29) And the Levite, (because he hath no part nor inheritance with thee,) and the stranger, and the fatherless, and the widow, which are within thy gates, shall come, and shall eat and be satisfied; that the Lord thy God may bless thee in all the work of thine hand which thou doest. (Deut. 14:28-29)

In Deuteronomy 26:12 (King James Version), it refers to the third year as "the year of the tithe", the third year tithe was to be spent in the children of Israel home town and the tithes were to be distributed to the poor. The other two years they had to travel or bring their tithe to a place the Lord would put his name to dwell. "When thou hast made an end of tithing all the tithes of thine increase in the third year, which is the year of tithing, and hast given it unto the Levite, the stranger, the fatherless, and the widow, that they may eat within thy gates, and be filled." The law of the tithe in Deut. 14:28-29, coincide with Deut. 26:12. Chapter 14:28-29, says, "At the end of three years thou shalt bring forth all the tithe of thin increase the same year, and shalt lay it up within thy gates: (v. 29) And the Levite, (because he hath no part nor inheritance with thee,) and the stranger, and the fatherless, and the widow, which are within thy gates, shall come, and shall eat and be satisfied; that the Lord thy God may bless thee in all the work of thine hand which thou doest."

It is sad to say, that widows on fixed income today are encouraged by some Pastors, ministers and evangelist, to give a tenth of their social security benefits to the Lord. It breaks my heart when I hear of senior widows who are in need of money to pay their light or gas bill, but instead will pay their tithes out of coercion or traditionalism. Today's tithing does not reflect the law of the tithe in Deut. 14:29. In verse 29, the tithe was for the widow, not only the widow, but the stranger and the fatherless and it was something you ate.

To make sure that no dishonest practiced existed for tithing, each Hebrew was compelled to make a declaration of honesty before the Lord:

> I have not eaten it in my mourning, neither have I taken away duty it for any unclean use, nor given duty of it for the dead: but I have listen to the voice of the Lord my God, and have done according to all that he has commanded me. (v. 15) Look down from thy holy habitation, from heaven, and bless thy people Israel and the land which thou have given us, as thou swarest to our fathers, a land that floweth with milk and honey. (Deut. 26:14-15)

Was there only one tithe each year or was the third-year tithe an extra one? There is still some confusion about this, even among Hebrew scholars. The tithe was indeed annual, according to Deuteronomy 14:22 (The law of the tithe): "Thou shalt truly tithe all the increase of thy seed, that the field beingeth forth year by year." Farmers produced crops once a year. However, as the need for funds increased with the expansion of the temple service, the

Mosaic Law required a third-year tithe (intended exclusively for the use of the Levites and those in need) was obtained as well.

To summarize, there are three tithes described in the Bible:

1. General tithes were paid to the Levites. "And, behold, I have given the children of Levi all the tenth of Israel for an inheritance, for their service which they serve, even the service of the tabernacle of the congregation" (Num. 18:21). The Levites were given 48 villages as their inheritance (see Numbers 34:16, 35:8, and Joshua 21 list the cities). The children Israel had to give a tenth of their tithes to the priest Aaron. "Thus ye also shall offer a heave offering unto the Lord of all your tithes, which ye receive of the children of Israel; and ye shall give thereof the Lord's heave offering to Aaron the priest" (Num. 18:28).
2. The tithe for the festal meal eaten by the offerer and his guest at the sanctuary (see Deut. 14:22-27).
3. The tithe paid every three years to the poor: the stranger, the fatherless, and the widow (see Deut. 14:28-29).

CHAPTER 10:
WHY WAS THE TITHE IMPLEMENTED?

Tithing was part of the law and the law was given because of the Israelites' transgression against God, they disobeyed Him by worshipping other gods. They were sinners and the law was given to convince them of their sin. The law governed what the children of Israel should and should not do. For instance, the law commanded if a man steal an ox or a sheep and kill it or sell it, he had to restore five oxen for an ox and four sheep for a sheep. The law was a temporary substitute until the promised seed had come, which was Jesus Christ. When the fullness of time had come, then the law as given to Moses was to cease. The Mt. Sinai covenant was a mutual commitment between God and Israel, with Moses being the mediator for the children of Israel. But the promise covenant God made with Abraham involved a commitment only from God's side; no mediator was involved. He made this promise to Abraham long before the covenant He made with the children of Israel. In Genesis 17:3-6 He says, "And Abram fell on his face: and God talked with him, saying, (v. 4) As for me, behold, my covenant is with thee, and thou shalt be a father of many nations. (v. 5) Neither shall thy name any more be called Abram, but thy name shall be Abraham; for a father to many nations have I made thee. (v. 6) And I will make thee exceeding fruitful, and I will make nations of thee, and kings shall come out of thee. Therefore, the law given by God had no affect on the promise He made to Abraham.

CHAPTER 11:
MONEY AND TITHES

I had people tell me that money is used today for tithes because they didn't have money back then. Apparently, these people have not read Exodus 30:11-16. Money was used for the atonement of the children of Israel souls.

> And the Lord spake unto Moses, saying, (v. 12) When thou takest the sum of the children of Israel after their number, then shall they give every man a ransom for his soul unto the Lord, when thou numberest them; that there be no plague among them, when thou numberest them. (v. 13) This they shall give, every one that passeth among them that are numbered, half a shekel after the shekel of the sanctuary: (a half shekel is twenty gerahs:) a half shekel shall be the offering of the Lord. (v. 14) Every one that passeth among them that are numbered, from twenty years old and above, shall give an offering unto the Lord. (v. 15) The rich shall not give more, and the poor shall not give less than half a shekel, when they give an offering unto the Lord, to make an atonement for your souls. (v. 16) And thou shalt take the atonement money of the children of Israel, and shalt appoint if for the service of the tabernacle of the congregation; that it may be a memorial to the children of Israel before the Lord, to make an atonement for your souls.

It is clear that the Israelites gave money (not tithes) as atonement for their sins. The half shekel was not a tithe, but an offering unto the Lord.

In understanding the Bible, one must understand for whom it is written and to whom it applies. I questioned how Bishops, Pastors, Ministers, Missionaries, or Evangelists could study the word of God and only use three or four scriptures to justify tithing. Before I give you those scriptures, I would like to refer to Genesis 13:2 (NIV Study Bible), in which Abram had become very wealthy in livestock and in silver and gold. This was not because he was tithing. Abram had become wealthy when he went down into Egypt during a famine. He had Pharaoh think his wife Sarah was his sister and Pharaoh entreated Abram with sheep, oxen, he asses, menservants, maidservants, she asses, and camels, read Genesis 12:14-16. (keep in mind he never paid tithes on his wealth.) I would also like to refer to Genesis 28:20-22 (King James Version), which states,

> And Jacob vowed a vow, saying, If God will be with me, and will keep me in this way that I go, and will give me bread to eat, and raiment to put on, (v. 21) So that I may come again to my father's house in peace; then shall the Lord be my God: (v. 22) And this stone, which I have set for a pillar, shall be God's house: and all that you shall give me I will surely give the tenth to you.

Notice that Jacob vowed to give God a tithe, provided the Lord allowed him to return back to his father's house safely. These scriptures are never used to encourage believers they owe God a tithe. Because in reading these scriptures, the reader will understand that it was the children of Israel who were the ones that were lead out of Egypt by Moses to journey to their promise land of Canaan. Prior to the children Israel possessing the Land of Canaan, they wondered in the wilderness for forty years because they disobeyed God and served idols gods. The Lord had given to Moses decrees and laws for the children of Israel to follow in the land He had given them to possess. One of these laws was tithing. The tithes were to be brought to a place for worship where the Lord would put His name to dwell. Deut. 12:1, 4-7 NIV says, "These are the decrees and laws you must be careful to follow in the land the Lord, the God of your fathers, has given you to possess—as long as you live in the land. (v. 4) You must not worship the Lord your God in their way. (v. 5) But you are to seek the place the Lord your God will choose from among all your tribes to put his Name there for his dwelling. To that place you must go; (v. 6) there bring your burnt offerings and sacrifices, your tithes and special gifts, what you have vowed to give and your freewill offerings, and the firstborn of your herds and flocks. (v. 7) There, in the presence of the Lord your God, you and your families shall eat and shall rejoice in everything you have put your hand to, because the Lord your God has blessed you."

Here are scriptures that some Pastors mainly use to justify tithing:

- "And Melchizedek king of Salem brought forth bread and wine: and he was the priest of the most high God, (v. 19) And he blessed him, and said, Blessed be Abram of the most high God, possessor of heaven and earth. (v. 20) And blessed be the most high God, which hath delivered thine enemies into your hand. And he gave him tithes of all" (Gen. 14:18-20, KJV).
- "Will a man rob God? Yet you have robbed me. But ye say, "Wherein have we robbed thee?" "In tithes and offerings." (v. 9) Ye are cursed with a curse: for ye robbed me, even this whole nation. (v. 10) Bring ye the whole tithes into the storehouse, that there may be meat in mine house, and prove me now herewith, saith the Lord of hosts, if I will not open you the windows of heaven, and pour you out a blessing, that there shall not be room enough to receive it" (Mal. 3:8-10).

Malachi 3:10) says, " . . . that there may be meat in my house . . .", not money. The food was to take care of the Priest, the poor Levites, widows, orphans and strangers. This gave glory to God because the people would thank God for providing food for them. God did not require money, but he did require thanksgiving, communion, fellowship and a relationship. Yes, God was being robbed of thanksgiving from the poor Levites, widows, orphans and strangers. He was also being robbed of communion, fellowship and relationship from those who were poor. If the tithe were supposed to be money, this would have been a good verse to mention money; after all, money was first mentioned in Genesis. Malachi was written 500 hundreds years after Genesis. It is amazing how this scripture is taken out of context and applied to others for the benefit of clergymen. One must ask when did God change the tithe from food to money? God is not a tax collector that pastors, ministers, and preachers have made him out to be.

- . . . Make an atonement for Israel, and for all the work of the house of our God" (Neh. 10:33). This offering was a symbolic ransom given as an offering unto the Lord by each man who was 20 years and older. Later Joshua used the annual contributions to repair the temple.
- "And to bring the first fruits of our ground, and the first fruits of all trees, year by year, unto the house of the Lord" (Neh. 10:35).
- "And that we should bring the first fruits of our dough, and our offerings, and the fruit of all manner of trees, of wine and of oil, unto the priests, to the chambers of the house of our God; and the tithes of our ground unto the Levites, that the same Levites might have the tithes in all the cities of our tillage. (v. 37) And the priest the son of Aaron shall be with the Levites, when the Levites take tithes: and the Levites shall bring up the tithe of the tithes unto the house of our God, to the chambers, into the treasure house. (v. 38) For the children of Israel and the children of Levi shall bring the offering of the corn, of the new wine, and the oil, unto the chambers, where are the vessels of the sanctuary, and the priest that minister, and the porters and the singers: and we will not forsake the house of our God" (Neh. 10:37-39).
- "And at that time were some appointed over the chambers for the treasures, for the offerings, for the first fruits, and for the tithes, to gather into them out of the fields of the cities the portion of the law for the priests and Levites: for Judah rejoiced for the priests and for the Levites that waited" (Neh. 12:44).

- "Then <u>brought all Judah the tithe of the corn and the new wine and the oil unto the treasures</u>. (v. 13) And I made treasurers over the treasuries, Shelemiah the priest, and Zadok the scribe, and of the Levites, Pedaiah: and next to them was Hanan the son of Zaccur, the son of Mattaniah; for they were counted faithful, and their office was to distribute unto their brethren" (Neh. 13:12-13).

CHAPTER 12:
THE PHARISEES

I have quoted many scriptures on tithing, of which, I don't believe many believers have ever read or they read through these scripture never giving thought to the meaning of these scriptures, as it relates to tithing. Messages are not given on these scriptures because the message would clearly reveal the true meaning of tithing, what it was, and it being required under the Mosaic Law for the children of Israel. Tithing was commanded until the children of Israel went into Babylon in exile. Earlier I mentioned the Pharisees were the ones to re-established or re-enforce tithing after the children of Israel came out of exile. Again, the Pharisees regarded themselves as "separated ones." It is unclear from whom they were separated; perhaps the common people and the non-Pharisaic Jews. It is believed that the Pharisees were the creators and shapers of early Judaism, but they were not a dominant party within Judaism. (Elwell, p. 913)

The majority of the scribes and lawyers believed in the ideology of Pharisaism, but not all Pharisees were legal experts. Primarily, the Pharisees were the guardians and interpreters of the law. The synagogue and the Sanhedrin were institutions of the Pharisees. The Pharisees were organized around the observance of purity and tithing laws. The Pharisees were only one of several sects that influenced developments within the form of Judaism that was practiced during the Hellenistic and Roman periods. (Elwell, p. 913)

This development of Judaism took place after the destruction of the temple and the exile of Judah in 586 B.C. Remember, when the children of Israel went into exile, tithing no longer existed. This episode in Jewish history created two separate forms of the religion: an Old Testament religion of Israel and the postexilic religion of Judaism.

During the Babylonian exile, Jewish religious life changed drastically. The Israelites were deprived of land, the temple, and priestly cultic ministrations. As a result, Judaism started to adopt non-sacrificial religious practices. Instead of gathering at the temple to offer sacrifices, Jews gathered in homes for the reading of Scripture, prayer, and instruction. The "blood sacrifice" (sheep and goats) had instead become a "lip sacrifice" (prayer and repentance). (Elwell, p. 637)

Israel held on to the law and the Torah in Babylon because Israel was assured of its divine calling and mission. Around the fifth century B.C. the "father of Judaism," Ezra the scribe, established religious reforms by appealing to the Torah. During this era many Jews came to believe the true Jews were vigorously, unflinchingly obedient to the teachings of Torah. (Elwell, p. 637)

Scribes became the priestly interpreters of the Torah; they set their own authoritative teachings. In the second century B.C. the Pharisees taught that the oral law carried the same authority as the Law of Moses. Jesus, on the other hand, denied that the traditions of men were equal in authority to the written law. Paul denied that man could be justified before God by obedience to that law. (Read Mark 7:1-23, Gal. 3) (Elwell, p.637)

The Priest and Levites existed during the OT period. The Priest were the descendants of Aaron, and were responsible for the conduct of worship. The Levites were supportive staff. They were responsible for the maintenance of the temple establishment and certain religious duties. (Elwell, p. 954) The Priest and Levites existence had been the religion of the temple. In 70 A.D., the destruction of the temple and the scattering of thousands of Jews from the land brought a sudden demise to the priesthood and Levites. (Elwell, p. 954) "Without the temple, their purpose was gone and their role as religious leaders in the Jewish community passed into the hand of the rabbis." (Elwell, p. 954)

Based on the teachings of Judaism, there is no set of beliefs upon the acceptance of which the Jew can find salvation. Some saw Jesus as a political threat. The gospel disputes between Jesus and the Pharisees centered primarily around the validity and application of purity, tithing, and Sabbath laws. The following verses offer examples of these disputes:

- "But when the Pharisees saw it, they said unto him, Behold, thy disciples do that which is not lawful to do upon the Sabbath day" (Matt. 12:2).
- "How much then is a man better than a sheep? Wherefore it is lawful to do well on the Sabbath days. (v. 13) Then saith he to the man, Stretch forth thine hand. And he stretched it forth; and it was restored whole, like as the other. (v. 14) Then the Pharisees went out, and held a council against him, how they might destroy him" (Matt. 12:12-14). Jesus is Lord of the Sabbath, so he could make the rules as to what was lawful and what was unlawful.
- "Then came to Jesus scribes and Pharisees, which were of Jerusalem, saying, (v. 2) Why do thy disciples transgress the tradition of the elders? For they wash not their hands when they eat bread." (v. 3) But he answered and said unto them, 'Why do ye also transgress the commandment of God by your tradition?' (v.4) For God commanded, saying, 'Honor thy father and mother: and, He that curseth Father or Mother; let him die the death.' (v. 5) But ye say, 'Whosoever shall say to his father or his mother, it is a gift, by whosoever thou mightest be profited by me;' (v. 6) And honor not his father or his mother, he shall be free. Thus have ye made the commandment of God none effect by your tradition. (v. 7) Ye hypocrites, well did Isaiah prophesy of you saying, (V. 8) "THIS PEOPLE DRAWETH NIGH UNTO ME WITH THEIR MOUTH, AND HONORETH ME WITH *THEIR* LIPS, BUT THEIR HEART IS FAR FROM ME. (V. 9) BUT IN VAIN THEY DO WORSHIP ME, TEACHING FOR DOCTRINES THE COMMANDMENTS OF MEN. (v. 10) And he called the multitude, and said unto them, Hear, and understand: (v. 11) Not that which goeth into the mouth defileth a man;

but that which cometh out of the mouth, this defileth a man. (v. 12) Then came his disciples, and said unto him, Knowest thou that the Pharisees were offended, after they heard this saying" (Matt.15:1-12)?

- "And when the scribes and Pharisees saw him eat with publicans and sinners, they said unto his disciples: How is it that he eateth and drinketh with publicans and sinners." (Mark 2:16)?

- "And then the Lord said unto him, Now do ye Pharisees make clean the outside of the cup and the platter; but your inward part is full of ravening and wickedness? (v. 40) Ye fools, did not he that made that which is without made that which is within also? (v. 41) But rather give alms of such things as ye have; and behold, all things are clean unto you. (v. 42) But woe unto you, Pharisees! For ye tithe mint and rue and all manner of herbs, and pass over judgment and the love of God; these ought ye to have done and not to leave the other undone." (Luke 11:39-42) Again, the tithe here were all agricultural produce that were required in the OT law, besides, Jesus new these Pharisees practiced the law. Have you ever wonder why Jesus was always rebuking the Pharisees and Sadducees? And why didn't Jesus tell the young rich ruler to give him a tenth of his possession, but instead told him to go and sell all he had.

It seems part of the conflict between Jesus and the Pharisees were obviously a difference between Jesus' claims about himself and his repeated disregard for observances, which the Pharisees believed were necessary symbols of reverence. The Pharisees could not reconcile Jesus' to support their own understanding of piety and godliness.

CHAPTER 13:
UNDER BONDAGE

I understand that some bishops and pastors might be concerned about how their church will survive if members don't tithe; church mortgages, utility bills, the Bishop's or Pastor's salary, and other expenses all cost money. But this is where faith comes in; bishops and pastors must have faith and rely on God just like they tell their congregation to have faith and trust God. This deception of having church members under bondage by paying tithes to meet their need is not justifiable. Even though churches have a lot of debt to pay, this does not justify the manipulation of scriptures to cause people to live under fear of being cursed by God. How can a bishop or pastor say he is living by faith when the offering system dictates a believer is commanded to pay tithes in the 21st Century? I really don't see how such a bishop or pastor is living by faith. For some pastors, church members both new and old are just a dollar sign. Christ dying on the cross is worth more than ten percent; you can't put a dollar amount on Him dying on the cross.

Again, tithing was never intended to be money. Tithing was something that was to be eaten under the law, which no longer exists. When it was mandated, tithes were used to take care of the Priest and people, not buildings. Galatians 3:13 reads, "Christ hath redeemed us from the curse of the law, being made a curse for us; for it is written, CURSED IS EVERY ONE THAT HANGETH ON A TREE." This scripture also applies to sacrificial offerings because Christ was the ultimate sacrifice. The new order of priesthood has been fulfilled by Christ. He is our one great high priest who lives forever and there is no need for any continuation of sacrificing animals. He became the one perfect sacrifice by offering up himself. Now there is no room for any other sacrifice or any repetition of sacrifices. In Christ, the priesthood and sacrifice have been brought to fulfillment and finality.

Today's sacrificial offerings are imposed by man, not God. Paul's instructions on giving are found in 2 Corinthians 9:7, "Every man according as he purposeth in his heart, so let him give; not grudgingly, or of necessity: for God loveth a cheerful giver." Each believer is to give as he/she has determined in his heart. If believers are giving under the threat of being cursed, this is wrong. People cannot give cheerfully if they are forced to give. Some Pastors are audacious and tell their congregation if they don't pay their tithes, they are not saved or they are condemned as a sinner. You can never repay God for sending his only son to a dying world. You give unto the Lord from your heart. What does tithing have to do with salvation?

I want to inject a little note about firstfruits. Prior to going into the land of Cananan, The Lord had told Moses to tell the Israelites to bring the first grain from the harvest to the priest. This was to acknowledge that all of the produce from the land came from God. These were looked as a pledge of the coming harvest and these firstfruits went for the support of the priesthood.

In the New Testament, Jesus is our firstfruit of all who die in the faith according to 1 Corinthians 15:20, "But now Christ is risen from the dead, and become the firstfruits of them that sleep." Believers are "a kind of firstfruits" of all God created, "Of his own will begat he us with the word of truth, that we should be a kind of first fruits of his creatures", (James 1:18). I wanted to speak a little about first fruits because some Pastors are now asking member to give (money) as first fruit.

God is tired of the auction offerings of various amounts of money and the bartering of his word. It does not impress him. He wants people to give willingly and cheerfully. I can't understand why believers are paying for a blessing in order to acquire things when the Bible clearly says we are of a royal priesthood; adopted into the royal family. We are blessed because we are the children of God. The heart of the matter is if we seek first the kingdom of God, then all these things will be added to us (see Matt. 6:33).

Why does it seem that the only way to get something from God is to pay for it? When you know who you are in Christ Jesus and understand that your spirit is integrated with the Holy Spirit and the spirit of our father, you will be able to liberate yourself from the bondage of the law.

Whether this teaching was done in ignorance or intentionally, it is not too late to ask God for forgiveness and start studying and teaching the truth about tithing. We must teach believers the principle of giving, not tithing. We must learn from churches that do not have a tithing system, but instead have willing members who give cheerfully.

We are living in a day where the words of Micah and Revelation are prevalent in churches:

- "The heads thereof judge for reward, and the priests thereof teach for hire, and the prophets thereof divine for money; yet will they lean upon the Lord, and say, is not the Lord among us? None evil can come upon us. (v. 12) Therefore shall Zion for your sake be plowed as a field, and Jerusalem shall become heaps, and the mountain of the house as the high places of the forest" (Micah 3:11-12). Matthew Henry (1961) puts it this way; "The most righteous cause shall not be carried without a fee, and for a fee the most unrighteous cause shall be carried. The priests' work was to teach the people, but they teach for hire, and will be hired to teach anything, which they know will please. The prophets divine for money. A man might have what oracle he would from them if he would but pay them for it".
- "Because thou sayest, I am rich, and increased with goods, and have need of nothing; and knowest not that thou are wretched, miserable, and poor, and blind, and naked. (v. 18) I counsel thee to buy of me gold tried in the fire, that thou mayest be rich; and white raiment, that thou mayest be clothed, and that the shame of thy nakedness do not

appear; and anoint thine eyes with eyesalve, that thou mayest see. (v. 19) As many as I love I rebuke and chasten; be zealous therefore, and repent. (v. 20) Behold, I stand at the door, and knock, if any man hear my voice, and open the door, I will come in to him, and will sup with him, and he with me. (v. 21) To him that overcometh will I grant to sit with me in my throne, even as I also overcame, and am set down with my Father in his throne (v. 22) He that hath an ear, let him hear what the Spirit says unto the churches" (Rev. 3:17-22). One must watch out for being blinded by conceitedness or self-delusion.

The challenge today's church leaders must face is to start teaching the truth about tithing and instead teach believers the principle of giving. It is giving and not tithing that is taught in the New Testament. It is the poor who gives to the rich in the name of tithing. How much a person gives is personal and no one else business. It is not as a result of pressure, coercion, manipulation or false promises. Christians are not supposed to give grudgingly or out of emotionalism or sensationalism. Jesus himself taught his disciples about giving in Luke 6:38, "Give, and it will be given unto you; good measure, pressed down, and shaken together, and running over, shall men give into your bosom. For with the same measure that ye mete withal it shall be measured to you again."

CHAPTER 14:
THE OLD COVENANT VS THE NEW COVENANT

The first bullet below depicts how Paul encouraged the Gentiles Christians to excel in their giving. He never mentions or encouraged them to tithe, but to be givers. The rest of the bullets are based on the book of Hebrews, which gives a comparison of the Old Testament Covenant and the New Testament Covenant. The reason I bring this up is because tithing is part of the Old Testament Covenant. The book of Hebrews was written to the Jewish Christians. The writer encourages the Jewish Christians to hold fast to their belief in Christ Jesus. The book of Hebrews stresses Christ being superior and His New Covenant. In the New Covenant, Christ is the mediator of the better covenant. The shedding of Christ blood on the cross is mankind ticket to eternal life. Hebrews 8: 6 says, "But now hath he obtained a more excellent ministry, by how much also he is the mediator of a better covenant, which was established upon better promises." The New Covenant is God extending his grace to the Gentiles as well. The new covenant is better than the old covenant because it rests on the power of Christ's atonement for the sins of mankind. Jeremiah prophesied of this new covenant, 31:31 KJV, "Behold, the days come, saith the Lord, that I will make a new covenant with the house of Israel, and with the house of Judah." The old covenant was under the law, which could not save anyone; it was God's moral outline for Israel to live by.

- The Apostle Paul's teaching to the Gentiles Christians about giving suggested, requested, encouraged and appealed to the conscience of Christians. One's giving should not be scrutinized. When the Pastors and Church leaders start equipping the Church with knowledge and understanding of giving, then churches will have givers like the Macedonians who gave according to and beyond their ability and gave of their own accord. This is described in 2 Corinth 8:3 NIV, "For I testify that they gave as much as they were able, and even beyond their ability." The Macedonian churches gave entirely on their own; without any one coercing them to give a certain dollar amount.

They gave themselves to the Lord first and then to Paul's ministry according to God's will. Paul encouraged the Christians of the Corinthians churches to be like the churches of Macedonians to excel in the grace of giving, not in tithing.

- "For this Melchizedek, king of Salem, priest of the most high God, who met Abraham returning from the slaughter of the kings, and blessed him; (v. 2) To whom also Abraham gave a tenth part of all; first being by interpretation King of righteousness, and after that also King of Salem, which is, King of peace; (v. 3) Without father, without mother, without descent, having neither beginning of days, nor end of life; but made like unto the Son of God; abideth a priest continually. (v. 4) Now consider how great this man was, unto whom even the patriarch Abraham gave the tenth of the spoils. (v. 5) And verily they that are of the sons of Levi, who receive the office of the priesthood, have a commandment to take tithes of the people according to the law, that is of their brethren, though they come out of the loins of Abraham" (Heb. 7:1-5 KJV).

- "If therefore perfection were by the Levitical priesthood, (for under it the people received the law), what further need was there that another priest should rise after the order of Melchizedek, and not be called after the order of Aaron? (v. 12) For the priest hood being changed, there is made of necessity a change also of the law. (v. 13) For he of whom these things are spoken pertain to another tribe, of which no man gave attendance at the altar. (V. 14) For it is evident that our Lord sprang out of Judah; of which tribe Moses spoke nothing concerning priesthood. (v. 15) And it is yet far more evident; for that after the similitude of Melchizedek there arise another priest, (v. 16) Who is made, not after the law of a carnal commandment, but after the power of an endless life. (v. 17) For he testifieth, THOU ART A PRIEST FOR EVER AFTER THE ORDER OF MELCHIZEDEK. (v. 18) For there is verily a disannulling of the commandment going before for the weakness and unprofitableness thereof (v. 19) For the law made nothing perfect, but the bringing in of a better hope did; by the which we draw near to God" (Heb. 11:11-19).

- "By so much was Jesus made a surety of a better testament" (Heb. 7:22).
- "Who needeth not daily, as those high priests, to offer up sacrifice, first for his own sins, and then for the people's: for this he did once, when he offered up himself. (v. 28) For the law maketh men high priests which have infirmity; but the word of the oath, which was since the law, maketh the Son, who is consecrated for evermore" (Heb. 7:27-28).
- "For every high priest is ordained to offer gifts and sacrifices; therefore it is of necessity that this man have somewhat also to offer, (v. 4) For if he were on earth, he should not be a priest, seeing that there are priests that offer gifts according to the law: (v. 5) Who serve unto the example and shadow of heavenly things, as Moses was admonished of God when he was about to make the tabernacle: for, SEE, says he, THAT YOU MAKE ALL THINGS ACCORDING TO THE PATTERN SHOWED TO YOU IN THE MOUNTAIN" (Heb. 8:3-5).
- "But now has he obtained a more excellent ministry, by how much also he is the mediator of a better covenant, which was established upon better promises. (v. 7) For if that first covenant had been faultless, then should no place have been sought for the second. (v. 8) For finding fault with them, he said, BEHOLD, THE DAYS COME, SAITH THE LORD, WHEN I WILL MAKE A NEW COVENANT WITH THE HOUSE OF ISRAEL AND WITH THE HOUSE OF JUDAH" (Heb. 8:6-8).

Jesus came to fulfill the Law and to give the law its full meaning, not to abolish or cancel it. Christ came out of the tribe of Judah, a tribe with no connection to the Levitical priesthood. The scribes and Pharisees were enemies to Christ and his doctrine. Jesus explained to his disciples that the religion he came to establish excluded the badness and included the goodness of the scribes and Pharisees. We must do more and better than the Pharisees did. They aimed for praise and applause of men, but we must aim for acceptance from God. We must deny ourselves of our self righteousness and say we are unprofitable servants and trust only the righteousness of Christ.

Believers are told to have faith in God and trust God with their tithing, even if their tithe money is their electric bill payment, the baby's milk or diaper money, or rent or mortgage money. Now the true test is whether the Bishops, Pastors, Ministers, Missionaries and Evangelists will trust God when believers no longer pay tithes, because believers will understand that the tithe was something to eat and not money and that it was commanded of the children of Israel in the Old Testament; Christ dying on the cross, no longer required the rituals of the Mosaic laws.

CHAPTER 15:
WHAT DOES THE NEW TESTAMENT
SAY ABOUT TITHING AND GIVING?

By the time of Christ, Roman rule had greatly affected the economic life of Judea; it was difficult for people to tithe. But the laws regarding the tenth were still observed, as is evident in the fact that the Pharisees even tithed the herbs that were used in seasoning food:

- "Woe unto you, scribes and Pharisees, hypocrites! For ye pay tithe of mint and anise and cumin, and have omitted the weightier matters of the law, justice, mercy and faith: These ought ye to have done, and not to leave the other undone." (Matt. 23:23).
- "But woe unto you, Pharisees! For ye tithe mint and rue and all manner of herbs, and pass over judgment and the love of God: these ought ye to have done, and not to leave the other undone." (Luke 11:42).

Those Pharisees continued to practice the Law even while Jesus was there with them and they did not give money as tithes. Jesus never once said that tithes are to be money. Instead he pointed out to the Pharisees how they had neglected the more important matters of justice, mercy and faithfulness. Jesus knew the Pharisees were the enforcers of the Mosaic Law, the law of good works which does not lead to salvation because it could not take away sins. Hebrews 10:11 says, "And every priest standeth daily ministering and offering oftentimes the same sacrifices, which can never take away sins." Again, the law was re-established after some of the Jews had returned from the Babylonian Exile. The Pharisees were the law enforcers who crucified our Lord Jesus. Again, good works do not lead to salvation, but the law of righteousness leads to salvation, and the Mosaic Law lead to sin because it made the children of Israel aware of their sins, but never took the sins away.

In chapter 18 of Luke, Jesus tells a rich young ruler to go and sell all he has and distribute the money to the poor. The rich young ruler becomes very sad because he was wealthy. Unlike pastors today who would have seen this as receiving a ten percent tithe from a rich young man, Jesus never tells the rich ruler to give him tithes.

When Jesus came, the children of Israel no longer needed to offer bulls and lambs, nor did they have to bring tithes (grain, new wine, oil and the first born of cattle) or meet the Lord at a certain place to worship, praise, and have communion and fellowship with him. The word was with them and they fellowshipped with the word (the Word became flesh). Jesus came to his own people, the Jews and they did not receive him. He had fellowship with his disciples and those who would come to hear him speak.

Jesus is our new priest; he is *not* under the order of Aaron's priesthood. In the Old Testament people brought their tithes to a designated place the Lord chose, whereas in the New Testament they had the privilege of fellowshiping with the Lord Jesus. This is why you never read where Jesus told the Jews to bring him their tithes, because he is the bread of life.

The New Testament does not imply that tithing is still relevant for today. I will go further to say that it does not indicate whether believers paid tithes while Jesus was with them. What the New Testament does say is that the Pharisees were the ones still observing the law. They continued to observe the law because their king had not come and they did not believe that Jesus was the Son of God.

Jesus never instructed his disciples or his followers to pay him tithes. If tithing was required, it would have made sense for Jesus to instruct his followers to tithe, but instead he instructed them to give to the needy and taught them parables about how to give. He let them know he did not come to destroy the law but to fulfill the law: to give the law its truest meaning.

Jesus says in Matthew 5:19-20, Whoever therefore shall break one of these least comments, and shall teach men so, he shall be called the least in the kingdom of heaven (it does not mean you won't make it to heaven, you will just be called the least in God's kingdom) but whoever shall do and teach them, the same shall be called great in the kingdom of heaven. (v. 20) For I say unto you, 'That except your righteousness shall exceed the *righteousness* of the scribes and Pharisees, you shall in no case enter into the kingdom of heaven.

Jesus was not pleased with the Pharisees and the teachers of the law. In his eyes, their interpretation of the law and view of righteousness was hypocritical. Jesus declares their righteousness must come through faith in him and his works. Our righteousness must exceed the righteousness of the Pharisees and the teachers of the law.

Jesus had told his disciples he had come to fulfill the law. In Matthew 5-6 he gives the truest meaning to fulfilling the law. He speaks about giving, but never about tithing. This would have been a good time for him to demand the continuance of tithing.

Again, only those hypocritical Pharisees and teachers of the law were still practicing the law. Their salvation was based on the law by works and not salvation by faith.

Throughout Jesus' ministry he never tells his disciples they have to pay tithes. Nor does he speaks about tithing except for when he criticizes the teachers of the law and Pharisees for giving a tenth of their spices: mint, dill and cumin.

When Jesus sent his disciples out, he instructed them not to go among the Gentiles or enter any town of the Samaritans, instead he told them to go to the lost sheep of Israel and peach the message: " . . . The Kingdom of heaven is near" (Matt. 10:7) In the 8th chapter of Matthew, he tells his disciples to heal the sick, raise the dead, cleanse those who have leprosy, and drive out demons. After he says that, he tells them, "freely you have received, freely give" (Matt. 10:8). In other words , don't charge anyone for what I have given to you for free.

In one of Jesus' sermons, he says, "Give and it will be given unto you; good measure, pressed down, and shaken together, and running over, shall men give into your bosom. For with the measure that ye mete withal it shall be measured to you again." In other words, it will be pressed down, then shaken together, pressed down, shaken together and repeated until it reaches the top and then it will run over. (Luke 6:38)

In Acts 20:35, before Paul's departure to Jerusalem, Paul quoted the words of Jesus, " . . . It is more blessed to give than to receive." Again, although Paul is responsible for setting up the Gentile church, he never mentioned paying tithes. He knew that living according to the law meant being under the curse of the law and believing salvation could be obtained by good works.

The Apostle Paul, who set up the church for the gentiles; never mentioned tithing. However, he did mention about giving according to what you purpose in your heart to give. He says in 2 Cor. 9:7, "Every man according as he purposeth in his heart, so let him give; not grudgingly, or of necessity: for God loveth a cheerful giver."

CHAPTER 16:
MY TESTIMONY

As a young child I was taught to pay ten percent of what ever I earned for my tithe, whether it was ten cents or a dollar. When I was around 14 years old, I stopped because it didn't make sense to me. I refused to pay tithes because I couldn't see the point of giving my money to the Pastor so he could spend it however he wanted to. A whole year went by before my dad realized I was not paying tithes. He came to me and asked me why I had stopped tithing, and I told him I didn't think the Pastor should not be able to do spend the tithes the way he wants to. My dad told me to continue to pay my tithes and not to worry about what the Pastor does with the tithes, saying, "That's between God and the Pastor." (I can only say that God must have been preparing me then for the writing of this book) I resumed paying my tithes, but when I was around 28 years old I stopped again. Even though I didn't pay tithes, I still gave liberal offerings: giving of my time and resources to help others, offering whatever help I could provide to others. I am truly a giver, and the Lord loves a cheerful giver. The blessings of the Lord were still being bestowed upon me and I never lacked.

Sometime in my 30s I started back-paying tithes. (Even the sound of "paying" tithes; or the phrase "you owe God your tithes" didn't feel right in my spirit): I found myself not paying tithes when I was around 46 years old; now I'm 50 and I have not paid tithes since. I thank God for liberating me from the bondage of the law. Earlier I mentioned, I was told at the church I use to attend; that I could not be part of the telephone prayer ministry, if I wasn't a tither. God knew if I thought I had to tithe in order to pray for someone, I would do an in depth study on tithing. I still have not found the scripture that says you have to tithe in order to pray for someone. I have not once regretted not paying tithes. Actually, my walk and fellowship with the Lord is even closer.

In 2006, I was laid off from my job at an aerospace company and worked as a temporary employee for another aerospace company for over two and a half years with no benefits. I never got paid for holidays and had no vacation days. When the company would have their Thanksgiving and Christmas Holiday plant shutdown, I didn't get paid (that was a loss of over $200.00 per day). Although I am married, we split our expenses down the middle. In addition to our house mortgage, we also have a second mortgage for a condo we purchased. I still had to give my share; I am not sure how I was able to still do my part, but I did. I can truly say Jehovah-Jireh is my provider. We never lacked and every bill was paid. Thank God.

As a temporary employee, I would still go on interviews because I wanted to become a permanent employee with benefits. There were a couple of interviews where I was told I had the job and I should let my current employer know I would no longer be working there. I thanked God for wisdom, because each time I told myself to wait until I you received the paperwork signed off. Inevitably, each time I waited for the paperwork, I would receive another call back saying they changed their mind or some other explanation. Before I could get disappointed or depressed, I would say to God, I know you have something better for me. Years ago, I learned to ask God to bless me with a job and let me know when it's time for me to move on. I didn't want a job just because it paid good money, I had that in the past and it was havoc everyday; I have learned to ask God to bless me with a job: the right job. In everything that I acquire, I have learned to say, God bless me with whatever that is because "The blessing of the Lord, it makes rich, and he adds no sorrow with it" (Proverbs 10:22). People would tell me they couldn't live like that, they would go crazy, but my trust was in the Lord and I would tell God, I totally trust you and depend upon you. When you have a relationship with the Father, He will not withhold any good thing from you. I want you to understand during this time, I did not pay tithes and I still do not pay tithes. I still gave and helped people and participated in events as if I had a full time job with vacation/holiday pay and benefits. In waiting patiently for the Lord to bless me with a permanent job, I finally got hired at a company that is government funded through 2025. I can only say that God has truly blessed me with this job because the day after my current employer hired me, the company I was working for had a 25% lay-off and the manager told me I would have been part of that lay-off. He was glad he didn't have to lay me off because I had given my resignation the previous night before I left work. God is good, good, good!

In the latter part of 2008, my husband was diagnosed with a serious disease, which lead to extensive treatments in 2009. Through prayer and the fervent prayers of prayer warriors, God has healed him. I was even diagnosed in 2009 with kidney damage and I have been healed because of the fervent and eventual prayers of the righteous. Some will say this happen to me, (even though God healed me), because I have not been paying my tithes. But I say this is life and being able to know God not only as Jehovah-Jireh, the Lord our provider, but also as Jehovah-Rapha, the Lord our healer. I know of saints who tithe and have lost their homes, jobs, and cars, or suffer from cancer, heart attacks, strokes, diabetes, and a plethora of other illnesses and diseases. So, my husband illness really could not have been because I was not paying tithes.

Although I am a License Evangelist, I started writing this book before I obtained my Evangelist License. I thank God for the opportunity to write a book that will liberate his people and no longer keep them in bondage.

REFERENCES

Baxter, J. S. (1960). *Baxter's explore the book*. Grand Rapids, MI: The Zondervan Corporation.

Douglas, J.D., & Tenney, C. M. (1989). *NIV compact dictionary of the Bible*. Grand Rapids, MI: The Zondervan Corporation.

Elwell, A. W. (Ed.) (2001). *Evangelical dictionary of theology* (2nd ed.). Grand Rapids, MI: Baker Book House Company.

Henry, M. (1961). *Matthew Henry's commentary*. Grand Rapids, MI: The Zondervan Corporation.

Nelson, T. (1988). *The King James study Bible*. Nashville, TN: Liberty University Press.

Zondervan. (2002). *NIV study Bible*. Grand Rapids, MI: The Zondervan Corporation.

NOTES

NOTES

NOTES

NOTES

Email address: willamanrobgod@gmail.com